STAND WITH ME

BY: CORBAN S. WALKER

STAND WITH ME

AN ANTHOLOGY OF FRESH PERSPECTIVE POETRY FOR A NEW SOCIALLY AWARE SOCIETY

CORBAN S. WALKER

"Flesh may not last, but the deeds of one's accomplishments in his lifetime will forever echo throughout the sands of time."

-C.S.W

With Special Thanks:

Rachel Walker (Mom), Michael Walker (Dad),
Jaden Walker (Lil Bro), Roylin Walker (Pop Pop),
Saundra King (Grandma), Essie Winn (Grandma),
Donna Ciccone, Nick Stambuli,
Patrick Verney, Asha Tyson,
Sister Souljah Jennifer Bailey,
Marshall J. Leak Jr. (Artist), Amina Troupe (First Moon)

Shouts outs:

To the Squad
My Social Media Family
The Muses

Much love to my Family and Friends who have supported
me along this journey!

Last but not least my Ancestors who continue to inspire
my creativity.

Foreword

You stole my heart the moment I knew you were in existence. Having you for a son is more than I could have ever imagined. I am so very proud of your accomplishments and this book of poetry is just one example. I know that greatness is ahead because of your laser focus matched with purposeful action.

I am so excited for you as you release your spirit in words to the world. I pray that every set of eyes and ears hear the messages you are broadcasting into the universe.

Rejoice Son, as your journey continues always remember your first "fan" is here for you past infinity!!

Love,
Mom

Table of Contents

ELEMENTS

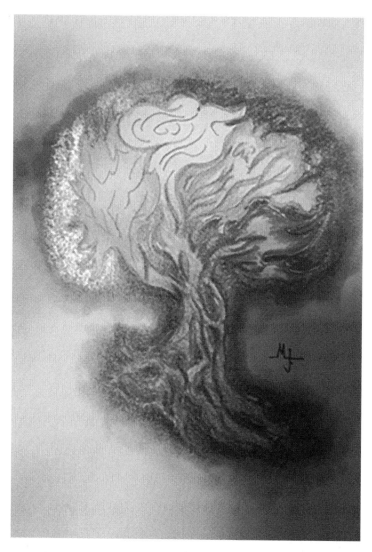

Rain

Rain drops lightly tapping the concrete
It's light rhythm bringing ease
The scent riding the cool evening's breeze

Freedom both bitter and sweet
Anxiety weighing down my
shoulders
The world's pressures acting as
boulders

At peace within the solitude of
my own thoughts
To be free
What does this mean?
Freedom a luxury of those who
can dream

To dream, to believe in a reality better than the one I live
To make my dreams a reality I have to give blood, sweat
and tears
The forging of a champion crafted over the years

Earth

Heat Rays
Set the sidewalk ablaze
The spine chilling thorns of winter fade
While the vibrant colors of spring parade
For what is nature if it is not beauty?
What is hatred without cruelty?
Man takes our mother for granted
Leaving her forever branded
Our misdeeds corrupting her slowly
Treated far from a trophy
When you throw that paper on the ground
Just remember how we are all bound

The Color of Things

Beauty lies in plain sight
From the cities glistening light
To the speechless countryside

Winter's fangs of ice receding
Spring's warms embrace never misleading
The sun bleeds warmth giving us summer
Fall painting a picture as the tree's change color

Color bringing life to our skies
Blue giving a majestic look to our seas
Green clinging to the ground
A reminder all life is precious

Man's eyes fixed on the stars
Looking up at what could be ours
Exploration and Expansion
A once great planet now too small
Its children now answering the universe's call

RHYTHMS OF
THE HEART

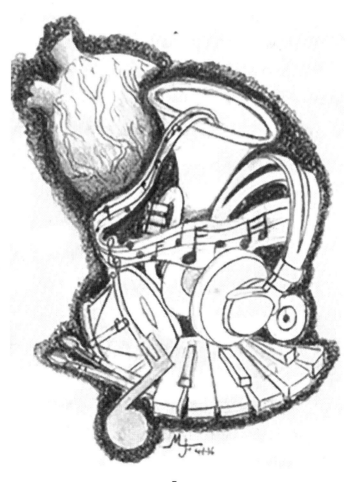

True Love

Started when I was young
Back when my head hung low
Needed it then, need it now
Overwhelming power forcing me to bow

Has me by the soul
Tried to stay clean, yet another failed dream
Who needs drugs?
When you have it

Dead in the night
I'm sweating in spite of my emotions
I cause a commotion as I run to the store
Crash through the doors as I see it
Reese peanut butter cups
My one True Love!

Heart Dilemma

See the same stuff everyday
See her and I don't know what to say
Do I take a risk?
Tell her she's the one I miss?
Do I stay quiet?
Still out of sight
Or do I just write about how I feel?
Yearning to feel something real

Nights in The East

Frigid winds patrol the streets
Night's shadow casting its ever expanding reach
The residents of the city put to sleep
City lights sweeping the restless concrete

When his thoughts aren't on his children they're of her
His wife's face becoming a blur
Love for his wife faded over the years
Arguments followed by tears

A loyal wife begins to realize her greatest fears
The man she has come to love has another lover
She shouldn't have to play big brother
A love reserved for no other

The adulterer's luminous skin free of age
Emotions kept locked in a cage
Her selfish tendencies kept at bay
A conflicted woman caught in the fray

A forbidden love never to see the
light of day
Night's shadow entertaining their
sins
Twisted love planting seeds within
A taboo love that can never win

Affairs of the Heart

Everyday life is a struggle
Night brings soft kisses and cuddles
I got an empty hole in my chest
Filled with shame and regret

Don't ask for much
The simple things and such
Full hugs real people someone that cares
But all I have is despair
Broken

One kiss and I'm floating on air
Hardly fair
Nothing worse than feeling alone
Guess I'll laugh when I'm grown

The Color of Love

Everyone got their kicks
See all I had was my wit
My source of power
Came not from some powder
Not from the bottle
Not from my crew
A young man searching for my inner truths

A red blanket was near
Reached for it
Tied it around my back
Superman style

Went from zero to Hero
With that Red blanket I felt strong
Gave me a sense of right and wrong
Protected me from my foes
Those who would see me fail

With Red by my side
We made em turn tail
I know it sounds stupid
But I concluded
Without that blanket I'd be nothing
Made me feel like something
A human being with a place in this world
That blanket was my mother
Would replace her for no other

Mina's Heartnotes

My heart flutters
From the moment you walk into the room
To the moment our eyes lock
To the moment your lips open
Til the moment you leave

Black excellence
An example for others to
follow
Our goals are their dreams
Two hands locked in unity
A well organized team

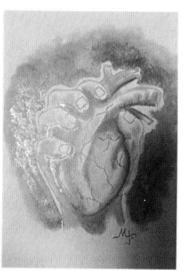

No No I'm a lone wolf
I`m supposed to be alone
But when I think of you my
imagination roams and
roams
For my emotions are real
A heart of ice now able to feel

The "L "Word

-

It's hard having a good heart
False promises, empty words
Thoughts of emotional warmth
Plaguing adolescent minds
Cuffing season

Being wanted
Wanting someone
Her hands gripping yours tightly
Striding through the halls like royalty
She is yours and you are hers
Full hugs followed by complete kisses
Unity

Quick to bond slow to understand
The L word used out of hand
Quick to unite, quick to fight
Two directions no exceptions
They didn't understand
Can't be forced or rushed
When it's time you'll know
When it's time everything moves slow
When it's time let it flow
Because no one is alone forever

Wonder

Wake up in the world
I'm just another face
Still searching for my place
Having on a poker face
Trying to avoid all things love
Caring only about the money
Made a habit of saying things bluntly
Everything changed
When I met her
Was smooth and clear
Now I live in fear
Of losing what we got
Deep in thought
In my twilight hours
Thinking bout her

Melody

They say the eyes are the
window to the soul
When I gaze at hers I lose
all self-control
Such beauty
Such passion
Words fall to rest as our
bodies take action

I love her
Words leaving her lips providing emotional warmth
A voice so soft it lightens the weight of the world
In times of need she's in your corner
Preaching message of inspiration and hope
When you're feeling down she's right there teaching you
how to cope

One must be careful of her wrath
A double edged sword able to cut both paths
Able to teach the Art of War over Compassion
It all depends on your course of action

I know her as Music
A force unlike any other
A unifier of man bringing together people from all over
A friend providing comfort, guidance, support and
motivation
I love her

Brothers

Coming from the same mother
A bond forming like no other
Deeper than blood
Stronger than the labels society has branded upon us
We are brothers

Summer nights filled with
misdeeds
Two brother take to the
streets
Setting down the controller
and letting their minds
roam
Two brothers not far from
home

Loyalty over everything
We are the one
Something not easily undone

Our back watched by one another
In the end we're all we got

In the end we are brothers

AWARENESS

P-ower

Power corrupts the hearts
of all men
Watched it breed a beast
within
It's claw digging into
innocents
It's howl shattering the
night
It's fiery gaze feeding on
your virtue
Be careful it may hurt you
Beware those who are
seduced
By its majestic beauty
The conqueror of souls
The bane of men
One can hold fast against
its lure
You will want to endure
Against the Arrogance
Deceitfulness
And selfishness
Stand tall against the darkness
Hold on to yourself or risk its consumption

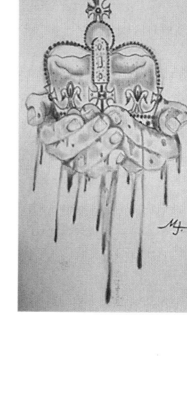

Want War

Hands trembling in anticipation
Hate pointed at the aggression of another nation
Excuses sought out to carry out our need for bloodshed
No thought about how many yet to be dead

Propaganda reaching desperate ears
Empty hands take to arms
A heroic calling set forth
A moral obligation to protect our farms

War is like fire
Once set don't let it burn for too long
It wears down both sides
Ravious fires as endless as the oceans tides

MSH 2012- 2016

High School
A mix of all sorts
Freaks & Geeks
Poor & Rich
Hoes & innocent souls
Where do I fit in?
Still trying to figure it out
One day I'll have it mapped it out
Call me divergent
Rumors and drugs spread like wildfire
Matters settled through gunfire
Fists and words
Absurd
Nas, Kendrick and Pac in my headphones
Mute the chaos
Not everybody gonna make it out
Only one gonna rule
In this chaotic high school

Wake Up

Tell ya somethin you already know
This world spins on dirty dough
Bills, Euros, Pesos
Kill em when I give the say so
Call that order 66

Genocide of the unlucky
In the eyes of the western powers
Diamonds pillaged from mother earth
Children die in the mines
While all we do is buy

All I have to worry about is school
Kids in El Salvador wondering who gonna rule
One day it will change
We know it's not fair
Just turn a blind eye cuz we don't seem to care
Just cause you shove trash in the closet
Doesn't mean it stops the smell
Hell I'm ringing a bell!

Old Soul

I look at the relationships between people in my generation and I'm taken by shock. How can people be so cruel and uncaring to one another? I've seen people cheat, lie, hurt one another physically and mentally. Is there any hope for love in a world appearing so cruel? What really upsets me is to see people within my own race treating each other as if dirt.

The men calling women "Bitches" and the women calling the men "Niggas", aren't we better than that? I've often considered myself an old soul (A gentlemen). If things don't change there will be a whole lot of middle aged unhappy people who don't understand how love works. Love is wanting more for someone than they want for themselves. A genuine respect has to be forged between the two before anything can take place. That means men treating women with the due respect they deserve, after all none of us would be here without them.

This means women treating men with the due respect they deserve also. Both genders whether they like to admit it or not both need emotional comfort. Too many people are caught up in body preferences. Whether they want women with curves or dudes that are ripped, they overlook possible options based on a biased opinion. If someone is a positive influence in your life and is willing to grow with you, you should give them a try. It's setting up a plan for future success. Find someone that will match your grind.

Manhood

From a young age young boys all around the country make the unfortunate mistake of attaching emotions to being "feminine". You don't need multiple partners to prove you're a "man". You don't have to be hard or be an emotionless hulking beast to be a man either. You don't have to be the strongest, bravest, best looking or richest. Often showing emotion is attached with a negative stigma. We aren't allowed to cry or show love in public.

The only emotion acceptable to display is rage or anger. We aren't allowed to give a compliment to our boys without attaching "No Homo" at the end. Being a man means taking care of your own and owning up to the actions you've carried out. I think where many people get their definition of being a man is from the media. The media saying you have to be physically strong, mentally and emotionally tough and a financial juggernaut. This is wrong each man should look to his inner truths to seek out a definition of what it means to be a man. After all everyone is different, how can we all hold ourselves to one view of what it means to be a man?

The Hollow

The second largest black enclave in my town
Neighbors more like family
Pushing through life together as if bound

Summer brings the most excitement
Hot days forcing you out of your home
Kids traveling together in groups
Old heads shooting hoops
Night brings mischief
Noise making and lust

Dirt bikes racing round the block
Word on the street says another life ended by the glock
But they say dealing is bad
His mother agreed when she saw her son laid out on that
slab

Ma raised me well
The streets I know are nothing compared to her hell
She's endured the worst of it
Yet to the sadness and grief she did not submit
So when I make these rhymes know it's for her I spit

RESPECT

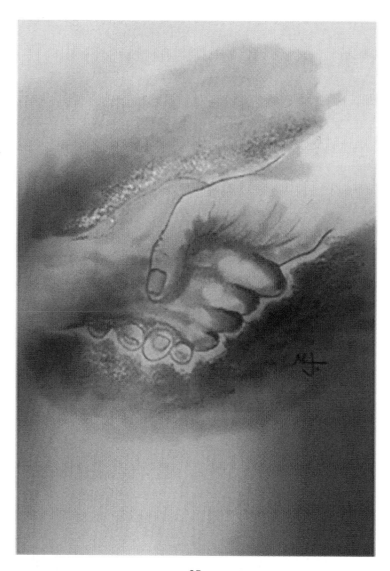

Blood on The Page

My people my people
Where have we gone wrong?
A once great people now sing such a morbid song
Such sad sight indeed victims another man's greed

Light-skin vs. Dark-skin
Poor vs. Middle Class Vs Rich
Referring to ourselves as Niggas to ("or) a Bitch
All things that keep us divided
A people now blinded to the truth
Taught to suppress the power that resides in you

Once rulers of a
majestic land
Now prisoners inside
our own minds
Ask yourself
When they own your
mind, pockets and spirit
Who needs chains?
When they make
choices for you, who
needs brains?
Servitude over
Ownership
Rejection of education

Mistreatment of one another
There used to be a time when we were all brothers
Victims of injustice
Voiceless occupants bearing witness
Whose words pass through America's ears with a
quickness

Venting my rage
Call that Blood On The Page

Because They Couldn't

I can because they couldn't
Not so long ago my people couldn't
Chained by the rules of society
We refused to be mistreated
A people refusing to be defeated

Public transportation
Able to take me to any location
From coast to coast, city to city, town to town
Any seat can be taken by me
A luxury taken for granted
I can because they couldn't

Education
Knowledge is power
When you control who has access to information
You can control the masses of any nation
Now I'm free to attend any institution
All thanks to their verbal revolution
I can because they couldn't

Not a victim of Jim Crow
Able to eat wherever I want
To walk around the town all nonchalant

Separate but equal?

More like the cutting off of a people
I can because they couldn't

Our heroes are all but gone
Unless they're able to spit bars or throw a ball
A new generation arises on the dawn
We have to finish what they started
To break the mental chains of slavery
Will require no small ounce of bravery
We can because they couldn't

Purpose

Inside there is something of vibrant light. Its presence can be seen within the depths of my eyes, felt through my actions. Though the outside world will try it's best to extinguish my flame I must stay strong and true to myself. When you make peace with what resides inside everything becomes clear...

Rage

Didn't go away with my age
Sharp pain in my rib cage
My life is far from hard
Still got my share of scars
See I'm different
An easy target for the ignorant
Though their words were insignificant
They still hurt
Made me feel like dirt
Forget my worth
Every dog has his day
I'm just waiting to fly away

Ode To My Ancestors

Africa forms my roots
Desert winds roaring over the land with ferocity
Jungles of luscious green, teeming with life
Snow decorating mountain peaks
The sun bestowing its warmth upon the land and its
people

Ancestors reaching out from beyond the grave
Speaking to a stolen son
Warning me not to forget where I'm from
Do them honor they say
Reach for the stars but remain down to earth

Know the strength that resides in your hands
Know the capacity of your intellect
Know the tenacity of your spirit
Know that our blood flows through you

They have tried to break you
Removing your culture, language, history and customs
Your struggle has not gone unseen, continue to dream
For one day the stolen son will return home

Rise & Shine

I walk in the shadow of a great man
Never acquired his taste for speaking
For what is a mouth?
If it has no words to spill
What good are emotions?
If you never feel
What are the purpose of eyes?
If they don't see
I'm just out here trying to be me
Mr. Walker
Come hell or high water
I'm going to make it
An industrial monster
So when you see me in ten years from now
Just remember how you made me frown
I'll be rich
Have everything I ever desired
The stars hold the key
And this is my destiny!

Lone Wolf

Keeping its distance from
those that can hurt him
The loner seeks to avoid the
eyes of others
Mistrust an emotion easily
seen within its eyes
Skeptical of any action thrown
in his direction

The wolf has always been alone
With others he has never roamed
Others are not to be trusted

The wolf observes their actions only to be disgusted
Staring at the moon he seeks guidance
Only to receive its everlasting silence
No longer belonging to a pack
A heart of ice never to turn back

The Ravishing

The beast knocks
Possessing a hunger knowing no bounds
Yellow bulging eyes filled with hate
A hungry beast knocks at the gate

Chills running down your spine
Hair standing to attention, goosebumps not far behind
Only you stand between the beast and its bloody crusade
Only you gripping the hilt of your blade

Live or die
Die or live
Look fear in the eye and it looks back
Let the beast have its way or fight
Let fear control you or conquer your fear

A beast knocks at the gate
Fear knocks at the corridors of our minds
What you do is for you to decide

PRIVATE
THOUGHTS

Immortal

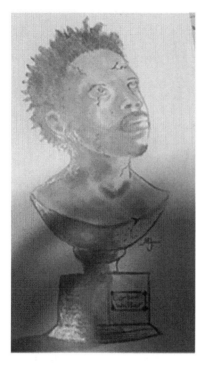

What's my goal in life? One may not live forever but names do. I want people to remember who I was, what I did and what I stood for.

Alexander the Great, Achilles, Hercules, these men died hundreds of years ago yet they live on through our tales of them.

That will be me….one day… Corban Walker will echo throughout the sands of time…..

Stand with Me

My invisible shackles cling in the night, I am not able to sleep.
Peer pressure, intimidation and lack of understanding forge my chains.

My views on life have often been called very "Black and White".
In my eyes the world is a bone-shivering heartless place where very few succeed.

In a country where the bad aspect of life are constantly blasted over the media networks, I find it hard to see any good.
News stations try to take advantage of current racial tensions to boost their ratings.

The richer get richer while the people like my mother have to break their backs every day to provide for their family.
I once said that we can't do anything to change things like that, I was wrong.

Someone just needs to take a stand I suppose.

Ghost in the Machine

Ghost in the machine
Sins haunting his dreams
There was a time when his humanity was intact
There was a time when the warrior found peace
This was before he put his foes to eternal sleep

He who walks alone
He who doesn't speak
He who doesn't sleep
The cost of his soul didn't come cheap

Words need not flow from his mouth
The evidence of past deeds branded on his rugged skin
No color is seen through his eyes
Only one priority seems to apply
Survive

Though he has the appearance of a man
Demons find shelter within
Fractured memories like splinters in his brain
The blood of his foes chilled upon his hands
The scent of the gunpowder never truly forgotten
No one knows how far he has fallen

He who walks alone
He who doesn't speak
He who doesn't sleep
He who seeks to find peace

Have and Have Nots

I was once told "There are two types of people in the world. The shoe shiners and the person getting their shoes cleaned". Sad thing is as I look over our modern society it seems to be true. The have and the have nots. The rich and the poor. Makes me want to be the best I can be. In the end I just want to build something that exceeds my own lifespan. I don't want to just be another face... Forgotten.

Every day I wake up thinking about my goals and aspirations. Thinking where I want to be 10 years from now. I don't have all the answers, but I do know Imma stick to being me and not trying to follow anybody.... Just a young man chasing his dreams I suppose

Society Washed

People have always been expendable parts to be used by the rich. People are born, go through the educational system then to a job where they work to make the dreams of another person a reality. After their value as workers has expired they retire and then die. Another person is born and the cycle continues. The people these workers spend a bulk of their life working for are the 1% that live as god's, being very wealthy. Choices are installed into everyday life to give the illusion of freedom. From a young age people are conditioned for their future role in whatever field they are to be deployed into. The media tries to distract us with the latest fashion trends, technology, sports games and celebrity beef, all to hide the fact that the working class are nothing more than slaves working for the benefit of their wealthy masters.

The rich own the government, its politicians being nothing more than puppets for vast corporations. People seem to forget that the world runs on money, but ask yourself whose pocket is the money in?

People are sheep afraid to be different and appreciate their individuality. They rather be told what to like, what to do and what to think. Let's be real it's easier to have someone giving you instructions than to actually think for yourself.

Thorns Of The Past

Watching a person revert back to their basic instincts is painful. This person that now stands before you is not what you remember them to be. A once sweet memory now tarnished by recent troublesome behavior. Still you have to try to remember the days when everything was alright. When you sat with them and laughed, smiled and have fruitful conversations. That's what you have to hold to hold onto in the end, the good times.

About The Author

Corban Shelton Walker Atlanta born. Jersey raised. Coming from a middle class suburban family, he's a young African American adult taking the world by storm through his words of wisdom. Graduating in 2016 he plans to attend college to pursue his ever-expanding dream of success and leaving a legacy of impact. Corban's interests are very diverse which includes fencing, music, writing, and raising awareness of social inequalities pertaining to minorities through social media.

Corban believes that change comes from broadcasting one's voice along with purposeful actions. His personal commitment to raising awareness has included participating in activist marches, social media campaigns and personal one on one interaction with diverse groups.

Corban is a well-rounded individual that is an avid reader, intense gamer and serious Sci Fi fanatic (Loves Lord of Rings, Matrix, Star Wars). He also believes educating the mind is not enough, but the body has to be up to par as well. When he is not writing or reading you can find him in the gym.

Corban believes family is everything and takes seriously his role as big brother and the oldest son in the Walker Clan. He is grateful for the support of his family and his friends and the opportunity to build legacy which for Walker, forms his immorality.

www.CorbanSWalker.com

About The Artist

Marshall J. Leak Jr.

Born November 1, 1982 in Orange, N.J., Marshall J. Leak Jr. is an artist and animator who explores the emotions of fear of life. He works primarily with computer graphics and mediums of art to produce work that addresses the nature of emotions and their role in defining reality. Marshall attended Gibbs College and obtained an associates degree in visual communications. He also studied 2D/3D animation and storyboarding at Bloomfield College. Marshall's biggest influence in his life is his father, who also loved art.